Work Less and Achieve More

Work Less and Achieve More

Table of Contents

Introduction 8
Things To Do Before Work 9
    1 Make a list of your tasks for the day. 9
    2 Check your agenda for the next few weeks. 9
    3 Use an app to keep track of your checklist. 9
    4 Set up reminders for meetings and tasks. 10
    5 Prepare all the materials that you need. 10
    6 Set your cellphone to silent or vibrate-only mode. 10
    7 Have a personal SIM and a work SIM. 10
    8 Choose neutral ringtones. 11
    9 Short message and reminder ringtones are best. 11
    10 Manage your e-mail settings. 11
    11 Proper work space setup. 11
    12 Check your tools and equipment. 12
    13 If you didn't do so the day before, tidy up. 12
    14 Distribute data and supplies. 12
    15 Check the evening news the day before. 12
    16 Eat a hearty breakfast. 13
    17 Prepare everything you need the day after. 13
    18 Have the proper mindset for work. 13
    19 Send out tomorrow's work today. 14
Things To Do During Work 15
    20 Check your inboxes regularly, not frequently. 15
    21 If possible, set an inbox notification sound. 15
    22 Focus! 15
    23 One task at a time. 16
    24 Learn and use shortcut commands. 16
    25 Get it right the first time, every time. 16
    26 Identify the time of the day where you are at peak performance. 17
    27 Take notes. 17

28 Tackle everything during the meeting. 17

29 Clear your mind as needed. 18

30 Get up and stretch regularly. 18

31 Complete communication tasks as early as possible. 18

32 Close all programs and browser tabs or windows that don't have something to do with work....... 18

33 Bookmark useful sites. 19

34 Organize your bookmarks. 19

35 Prioritize work as needed. 19

36 Install a good antivirus program. 20

37 Scan all files that you load onto your computer. 20

38 Keep your virus definitions up-to-date. 20

39 Keep your private info private. 20

40 Minimize open windows and applications.. 21

41 Save regularly... 21

42 Ask for UPS, or get a small one for yourself.. 21

43 Keep regular backups. 22

44 Keep detailed information on backups. 22

45 Keep records and store them properly. 22

46 Perform regular maintenance for your work computer. 23

47 Assign priorities... 23

48 Don't procrastinate. 23

49 Let yourself be seen. 23

50 Organize productivity contests 24

51 Propagate communiqués 24

52 Update your agenda or schedules as needed... 24

53 Maintain good relationships at work. 24

Things To NOT Do During Work 26

54 Don't seek entertainment during your work time.. 26

55 Don't distract yourself. 26

56 Don't let others distract you. 26

57 Don't download and install with abandon.. 27

58 Don't stream videos or download using the company bandwidth........................ 27

- 59 Don't visit websites other than reference and work-related websites. 27
- 60 Don't socialize during work. 28
- 61 Don't meet someone out of the blue. 28

Things To Do After Work 30
- 62 Put away your tools and equipment. 30
- 63 Shut down your computer. 30
- 64 If you need to leave your computer running, turn off the monitor and use an automatic shutdown application. 31
- 65 Tidy up your workspace. 31
- 66 Lock up. 31
- 67 Review your work at the end of the day. 31
- 68 Pat yourself on the back. 32

Things To Do In General 33
- 69 Find a way to unwind after work. 33
- 70 Put some good music on. 33
- 71 Get out of bed before the rest of the world. 33
- 72 Do not drink your stress away. 34
- 73 Perform regular maintenance on all tools and equipment. 34
- 74 Find out if anything's expired. 34
- 75 Check for discrepancies in inventory. 35
- 76 Mix in with the right crowd. 35
- 77 Perform financial audits. 35
- 78 Find time to exercise. 35
- 79 Get some well-deserved R & R. 36
- 80 Get enough sleep. 36
- 81 Make yourself comfortable. 36
- 82 Stay "electronic." 36

Things That Home-Based Workers Can Do 38
- 83 Establish a routine. 38
- 84 Find out when you are most ready for work. 38
- 85 Plan ahead of work. 39
- 86 Itemize your workload. 39

87 Tell friends and family that you are on work mode. 39

88 Focus but not on social networking sites. 40

89 Track your progress. 40

90 Set-up a home office or a separate space for work. 40

91 Outsource some of the work. 41

92 Buddy up and check on each other. 41

93 Invest in sound and reliable technology. 41

94 Modern conveniences are your best friends. 42

95 Take frequent and short breaks. 42

96 Dress for the occasion. 42

97 If you are not up to it, STOP. 43

98 Quantity or quality? 43

99 Do not burn yourself out. 43

100 Get a change of scenery. 43

101 Suit yourself. 44

Conclusion 45

Resources .... **Error! Bookmark not defined.**

Introduction

Productivity is a word that tends to get thrown around a lot, but most middle managers only use it in sentences asking the average employee to hunker down and get to it. Few people actually give you tips on how to achieve that quality of being able to produce good results consistently from your work.

In the modern world, productivity is a common ideal. It does not have to be the measure of much work you can accomplish in your job. Productivity can also be about completing the things you need to do at home, or even during your leisure time. The point is that you can get more things done in the same time or even less.

Without further ado, we present 101 quick productivity tips that you can apply to your daily life. Note that while we used the word "work" here, in practice these tips can be used to organize and slap rockets onto your home and social life. And so, we begin.

Things To Do Before Work

This section presents tips that are intended to help you complete your tasks in an organized manner through proper preparation. "Fortune favors the prepared mind", as Louis Pasteur said, so keep that quote in mind as you peruse this array of pre-work prep tips.

1 Make a list of your tasks for the day.

A simple checklist of the things you need to do can be surprisingly helpful at keeping you on track. Aside from ensuring that you don't forget to do any of the written tasks, when you see how much left you have to do, you can get serious about work. This can also help you avoid forgetting something and embarrassing yourself.

2 Check your agenda for the next few weeks.

There are times when tasks that have deadlines weeks from the current date will require preparation. As such, it is the best policy to always know what you should be doing within the next few weeks, so you can manage your time and resources properly. Remember to stay flexible, as changes can happen within those few weeks.

3 Use an app to keep track of your checklist.

If you have a smartphone, put it to work and use it to keep track of the things that need doing for the day. Apps like these can also help you prepare your schedule for weeks in advance. Remember that a smartphone is only as smart as the person who is using it.

4 Set up reminders for meetings and tasks.

When you set up a reminder on your cellphone, you are reducing the risk that you will run late or miss appointments and tasks altogether. Setting a reminder can also take a load off of your mind and allow you to concentrate better on the task at hand. Do make sure that your reminder ringtone won't bother nearby people, or you could be lessening their productivity.

5 Prepare all the materials that you need.

Though arguably this can be considered part of the work that you do, for argument's sake let us put it in this category. Having all the tools and supplies close at hand makes it easy to complete tasks because you won't have to break your concentration (or spend time) going to get something.

6 Set your cellphone to silent or vibrate-only mode.

Loud ringtones don't just break your concentration but also that of the people around you, unless you have your own office or something to that effect. Besides, it would be a bit embarrassing if you were surprised by your own cellphone. We don't quite recommend turning your cellphone off because there may be urgent matters that can only come to your attention through your cellphone.

7 Have a personal SIM and a work SIM.

If you can afford it (and if you have a high volume of message / call traffic on your cellphone), then get different SIM cards for your work and personal lives. You could put them in different cellphones, or on a single dual SIM phone, or just swap them in and out as needed. The idea is that you pay attention when the work phone rings, and can choose to ignore the personal phone until you have the free time to check it.

8 Choose neutral ringtones.

This is a little less obvious. Using humorous ringtones or ringtones that carry some sort of emotional significance for you can be distracting. It can also bother nearby people. Using "neutral" ringtones – ringtones that simply notify and do not entertain – means that there won't be emotional baggage with every ring, and you're less likely to bother other people.

9 Short message and reminder ringtones are best.

Ringtones that last a few seconds at most are best. Imagine if you left your phone on your desk while you stepped away for a bit, and a message came in. A long ringtone for a message that will be waiting when you get back is sure to annoy your coworkers. Choose something short.

10 Manage your e-mail settings.

Setting a filter to redirect and categorize your e-mail messages can be helpful, especially if you use one e-mail address for your work and personal life (which is not recommended, especially if it is a corporate e-mail address). This way if something pops up in the personal e-mail inbox, you can let it slide 'til later, while something that comes into the work inbox deserves at least a cursory glance.

11 Proper work space setup.

While having your own cubicle means that you can usually add things that express your individuality, adding too much personality to your workspace can be distracting. How can you focus on that spreadsheet when a poster of your favorite actor or actress is but a few feet away, tempting you with their paper gaze? Here's the tip in a nutshell: Decorate your workspace only with things that help you stay focused on the job.

12 Check your tools and equipment.

Whether you work in a cubicle or in a greasy garage, you should always check your tools and equipment before starting work. That way you can ensure that you won't waste time while in the middle of something important later on. Additionally, performing basic checks every day can prevent serious injury or equipment damage by allowing you to identify potential problems before they fail catastrophically. It will also keep you from embarrassing yourself by calling I.T. when your computer is simply unplugged.

13 If you didn't do so the day before, tidy up.

There are times that you might end up going home without cleaning up your workspace. While this is sloppy, it is also sometimes unavoidable, especially during crunch periods. In any case, if you come into work after having left your space dirty the day before, your first order of business should be to tidy up in preparation for the day ahead.

14 Distribute data and supplies.

People can't do their jobs if they are not supplied with the data and supplies that they need. If there are supplies or data that needs to be distributed to various personnel, then it should be done as early as possible. Just make sure to check your inboxes to see if there are instructions that say otherwise or make corrections before going about distributing whatever needs to get to the concerned parties.

15 Check the evening news the day before.

Every moment you spend not working are points against your productivity. This is why getting stuck in traffic is really a bad thing for anyone doing the daily grind. To avoid this scenario, check the evening news for any announcements for the day after. You will never know when they will close off some streets in your commute to work unless you check. This prevents the stress that comes from knowing that you are getting to work late in the morning. In case such an announcement is made, plan your route accordingly for a smooth commute to work and a better disposition in the morning.

16 Eat a hearty breakfast.

Low energy and a bad mood in the morning are often the results of skipping the most important meal of the day. Make it a point to eat your breakfast before going to work and you will see the difference. Drop the coffee-and-donut routine and look for something healthier like some fruit pancakes. No time to prepare in the morning? Make breakfast the night before and put it in a plastic container so you can eat it on the way. Just do not forget to pop it out of the refrigerator before you leave for work.

17 Prepare everything you need the day after.

In the morning rush to get to work the following morning, it is easy to forget things needed for work. It is not a big deal if you can easily replace them but what if it was your PowerPoint presentation outlining company performance to be presented to the top brass? This is a worst-case scenario the must be avoided at all costs. Do this by taking time to prepare everything you need before you go to bed. Make a list and check it twice before you doze off.

18 Have the proper mindset for work.

Sometimes, all it takes is the proper mindset to keep working. How could you finish that report when your mind is wandering? With this in mind, it is best to prepare your brain for work the night before you go to the office. When it is finally time to work, you will go straight to business without wasting precious time to motivate yourself while the clock starts ticking.

This means you have more time to finish your work and thus increasing your output.

19 Send out tomorrow's work today.

If you have subordinates, you can help them become more productivity by giving them their allotted work tomorrow on the previous afternoon. This lets them plan the next work day and think of how they go at it. In other words, you are helping them work more efficiently by giving them the opportunity to see what they are up against. So help your team become more productive and produces better results by giving them a sneak peek on the days ahead. This helps overall performance as well as boosts intra-office relationships and teamwork.

Things To Do During Work

This section covers the various productivity tips that apply while you are working. Everything seems rather obvious and common sense here, but the fact is that a lot of people need to be reminded of these things.

20 Check your inboxes regularly, not frequently.

There's a difference in checking your inbox at set intervals and checking your inboxes whenever you get the chance. Checking your inboxes, whether e-mail or phone, involves little time and few actions, but the distraction can be enough to lower your potential. This is especially true if you are the type who checks inboxes almost obsessively.

21 If possible, set an inbox notification sound.

In cellphones this is easy, but for e-mail it can be a little tricky. However, if you can set your e-mail program or system to make a notification sound when something comes in, you can skip checking your inbox unless it sounds. Again, the usual guidelines for ringtones apply – choose neutral, not too loud, and not too long.

22 Focus!

You might say "Well, duh" or something similar. However, no tip is too small or obvious in the pursuit of productivity. Concentration is both a talent and a skill. Some people can focus on tasks easily – they're usually the more productive ones – and some are not quite as good. However, you can train yourself to keep your cognitive and processing resources on the tasks at hand. It takes practice and, semi-ironically, concentration to build up your powers of concentration.

23 One task at a time.

Though the human brain is capable of handling many tasks at a time the cognitive part of it works best on just one thing at a time. Just like how a computer slows down when there's too much going on, your brain is not as efficient when there are several tasks to handle at any given time. Worse, you are more likely to commit errors than a computer is, especially when you attempt to multi-task. The bottom line: One task at a time.

24 Learn and use shortcut commands.

All software needed to finish the job come with built-in shortcut commands. While the standard point-and-click method works, using shortcut commands is a more efficient alternative. Simple keystrokes can work like magic and improve your output by a lot. The less time you have figuring out which menu to pull down, the more time you will have to finish up. Also, take a good look at your keyboard. Chances are there are already pre-programmed buttons that launch certain applications from the get-go. Familiarize yourself with these shortcuts and you will make better use of your computer.

25 Get it right the first time, every time.

This is strongly related to the previous tip. When you focus on just one task at a time, you are less likely to make mistakes. Also, you should regularly check and double-check your work as you go through it, not just at the end. Every mistake can mean that you will need to redo a section, or at worst, the whole thing. Productivity is as much about ensuring the quality of each output as it is about completing as many items as possible.

26 Identify the time of the day where you are at peak performance.

Just like TV has prime time, there is also a certain time frame where you are at your best. You can concentrate the most, able to work faster and more efficiently and produce better results during these hours. Do yourself a favor and make the most out of your prime time and really work into overdrive. The most difficult tasks of the day should be done when you are at your best. Anything that requires less attention should be moved to other times of the day.

27 Take notes.

Whatever it is that you do, don't forget to take notes of significant things. For example, if you come across some possibly important bit of information, make a quick note regarding its location and content. That way, you can put it out of your mind until the time you need it. Keeping your mind as free of clutter as possible makes it more efficient; the same principle applies to relegating reminders to your smartphone rather than your internal active memory. You might find that this technique also reduces the number and intensity of headaches!

28 Tackle everything during the meeting.

Getting up and out of your desk and asking your coworkers about work-related things are not only bad for your productivity but theirs as well. It is a complete waste of time and should be avoided as much as possible. This is why the time for meetings should be used for asking questions and making things clear with your coworkers. The more frequent the meetings the better it will be for everyone. Schedule meetings on Thursdays or Fridays instead of Mondays to avoid burning out your employees at the start of the work week.

29 Clear your mind as needed.

It does not have to be some exoteric Zen trick. Simply pausing your thoughts and taking deep breaths for a few seconds is enough to lower your blood pressure and clear your mind of clutter. If you find yourself getting confused or having a headache, pause somewhere you can easily pick up, and take a few moments to re-center yourself.

30 Get up and stretch regularly.

You might think that getting up keeps one away from work and distracts from the task at hand, but think again. When you get up and stretch, you relieve stress on your body and mind. With fewer distress signals to bother it, your brain can become more efficient than it could have if you just slogged through the aches. The trick is to pause your work in a way that you will find it easy to resume from. If your work was a set of math problems, then you should pause after completing a problem, not while in the middle of one.

31 Complete communication tasks as early as possible.

Communication is essential in any work, especially if it is a team project. Remember that others may be waiting on your output, or they need to be informed of changes immediately. By completing communication tasks early and quickly, you can ensure that the whole team stays on track. Send files and data as soon as you have finished checking them, and respond to inquiries in the most prompt manner possible.

32 Close all programs and browser tabs or windows that don't have something to do with work.

Your workplace is not the place to be harvesting digital crops or feeding virtual fish. Or at least, not during your active work time. If you can't just leave your games for after work, then do it during your breaks, not while you are working. Even better, don't play games while at work!

33 Bookmark useful sites.

If you use the Internet a lot while at work for work purposes, then keeping bookmarks for useful websites can be a big help. For example, if you find a great reference site, keep a bookmark of its homepage. That way, you can visit it again easily the next time you need to look something up. Even when you come across a site that isn't useful at the moment bur may prove useful in the future, add a bookmark to your Web browser.

34 Organize your bookmarks.

Aside from creating bookmarks, you should also keep them organized. Categorize them for easy lookup. File away old bookmarks that are no longer being used, or simply delete them. The idea is to make the bookmarks that you need easy to find by reducing the number of things you go through, either by deleting unused items or by grouping them for shorter sets to search through.

35 Prioritize work as needed.

Sometimes, work just keep piling up until you have a full stack on your desk. Of course there is nothing more discouraging than a stack of paperwork on your desk. If it does happen, approach the problem by doing work one at a time. Prioritize work according to what is more urgent and/or important. Anything that can be put off for later should be put off for later. When you are done with everything marked "Urgent," use your remaining time you have to tackle papers you still have left. This is a more efficient way of dealing with a stack of papers on your desk.

36 Install a good antivirus program.

Unless your IT administrator forbids installation of unauthorized programs, installing a good antivirus program should be top on your pre-work list. There are a few good free antivirus programs, but if you want premium protection then you might want to ask your administrator about a corporate installation of high-grade antivirus suites. A virus infection can cripple your ability to work, so it must be avoided at all costs.

37 Scan all files that you load onto your computer.

Before you even think about opening up removable media or files downloaded from the Internet, always run a context menu scan. Assuming you have an antivirus program installed, right click the file or file group and look for something like "Scan file". This should run a quick scan on demand specifically on the selected file or files. If it turns up clean, well and good. If it turns up infected, you'll want to quarantine or delete the file as soon as possible.

38 Keep your virus definitions up-to-date.

New viruses are coming out all the time, so if you want to stay protected, you should keep your virus definition databases up-to-date, if not up-to-the-hour. Most antivirus programs do this automatically, but only if they are set to do so (which is the default). Without the data, your antivirus software may not be able to recognize a viral infection. Bottom line: Make sure your antivirus program's database is updated and set to update automatically.

39 Keep your private info private.

This goes with little saying, but protecting your privacy and online financial security is strongly reliant on how well you protect your financial and personal information online. Make sure to read privacy agreements whenever possible. Avoid giving out credit information unless you can verify that the webpage you are on is what it is supposed to be, and not a look-alike. Checking the security certificate is a good way to lessen the likelihood that you'll end up giving away information to unsavory parties. And besides, you really should not be doing your online shopping while at work! Your company might be using software to monitor your behavior, which may include monitoring keystrokes – in essence, an untrustworthy workmate with access to the monitor data dumps can pick out your password or whatever important information you typed in.

40 Minimize open windows and applications.

This one applies to those who work primarily with computers. Avoid leaving too many windows and applications open, especially if your terminal is on the lower end of the specification spectrum. Not only will it slow down the performance in general, but you increase the risk of unresponsiveness and automatic program termination. That means data loss and wasted time.

41 Save regularly.

Not all programs have auto-save features, and those that do may not be set to save often enough. A sudden program freeze or crash can be troublesome, but the impact can be reduced by ensuring you save regularly. Manually saving about every five minutes (or setting the auto-save to that interval) is a good way to minimize data loss in case of unexpected program or system shutdown.

42 Ask for UPS, or get a small one for yourself.

UPS stands for Uninterruptible Power Source, which is basically a smart encased battery that automatically kicks in when the power goes out. Unlike a backup generator system, UPS activates instantly – perfect for computers which can cut out with power interruptions of mere fractions of a second. In fact, one could argue that a UPS never actually kicks in because it's always feeding power to whatever's plugged in – it's just that when the electric current is on, it continuously replenishing the onboard battery. A

UPS can give you enough time to save all your information and do a proper shutdown, ensuring you do not lose data and avoid potential system or program corruption.

43 Keep regular backups.

Keeping backups of your files and regularly updating those backups is one secret to productivity. It does add overhead and can be a little tedious, but you will surely not regret it when you lose the active information. Keeping multiple backups is also a vital practice for programmers, since they may want to roll back changes due to unforeseen circumstances. Your backups should be on a separate machine, remotely hosted, or on physical media that is stored properly.

44 Keep detailed information on backups.

You might know what's currently on your active files and maybe the most recent backup, but what about the backups before that? Having lots multiple backups can make it confusing and difficult to track down the one you want, so you should maintain a readable file that details the contents and changes found in your backup files. If you have enough space, you can keep backups for years to come, and that can mean lots of duplicate files that may not necessarily be the same. Avoid wasting time on finding the right backup by keeping a summary file.

45 Keep records and store them properly.

For any kind of work, maintaining records of important daily information is very helpful. This does not just improve accountability and the ability to recover from loss, but it can also help you monitor performance and take appropriate actions. Remember to regularly relocate your records to some secure location, safe from the elements.

46 Perform regular maintenance for your work computer.

Not all the required maintenance work for your computer has to be handled by the IT Department. There are actually a few things that are simple enough that you can do them on your own. For instance, deleting unnecessary files are just a few simple clicks away. Defragging can help your computer de-clutter its hard drive and keep it running at optimum speeds. Do this regularly like once a week and you will have a reliable computer to work with. No need to keep calling the IT guys and stop working altogether.

47 Assign priorities

Know how to quickly review tasks and use your foresight to arrange them and assign priorities. Priority values rely on metrics like difficulty, time to deadline, required resources (including time), and if you play office politics, who it's for. High-priority items should be worked on first, unless they rely on some as-yet unavailable resource. If a high-priority item cannot be worked on yet, turn to other high-priority items before taking care of low-priority items.

48 Don't procrastinate.

Don't put off work that you can do now. Unless something urgent that requires immediate attention comes up, you should direct your energies to completing whatever it is that can be done at this moment. Aside from lowering your overall productivity, procrastination sets you up for dangerous crunches that could be much less taxing if you completed your tasks as they came up.

49 Let yourself be seen.

This one is for supervisors and middle managers of all kinds. If you have a bit of free time on your hands, take a walk around and peek into cubicles and work stations, or at least act like it. Better yet, do it at random times. This will keep your underlings on their toes and can discourage tomfoolery in the workplace, increasing productivity.

50 Organize productivity contests

This is another one for managers and works best in companies which deal in products made or assembled by people. Organize contests with prizes and you might see an increase in overall productivity as the floor personnel get fired up trying to win that prize. Though in reality they should be putting in effort anyway, a little incentive now and then is not a bad thing.

51 Propagate communiqués

If there are instructions or other information that needs to be communicated to others, then it should be done as soon as possible. If it is your responsibility to do so, then make sure to take care of it right away.

52 Update your agenda or schedules as needed.

When changes occur that will have effects on schedules or your agenda, update your reminders, and if needed, communicate with the concerned parties. Do these as soon as the need arises so you don't forget to do so. This will help you avoid situations where you forget appointments or you don't get what you need because it was not requested beforehand, which causes stress and loss of time for everyone involved.

53 Maintain good relationships at work.

Being cordial around officemates is good not only for your productivity but the office as a whole as well. It is no secret that a harmonious relationship among coworkers promotes an efficient work process which is more likely to produce better results. Compare that to an office where a few coworkers are cold towards each other. In such extreme cases, it might even start hostilities among coworkers. Do you get why there is an annual company retreat now? If you are really not the friendly type, at least give your coworkers a smile every now and then.

Things To NOT Do During Work

Just like there are things that you should be doing during your work time, there are also things that you must avoid doing. This quite obviously includes things labeled as NSFW, but there's quite a bite more too.

54 Don't seek entertainment during your work time.

Unless it is your break time, you should not be doing anything that isn't part of your work. That means that seeking entertainment, whether online, offline, or on mobile devices, is discouraged as these can interfere with your work. Even if you use them during break time, you risk lowering your productivity should the content get stuck in your head, making you anticipate the next time you can enjoy that entertainment.

55 Don't distract yourself.

It's too easy to get lost in all the stuff that's online, or on your mobile devices, especially if the company you work for is not very strict about the use of the company Internet bandwidth. Sooner or later, you end up looking through LOLcats or following the adventures of webcomic characters – unless of course you have the discipline to stick to what you're supposed to be doing. Stay focused on your work, and whatever you do, don't click that mysterious link!

56 Don't let others distract you.

Sometimes the mystical allure of LOLcats and viral videos comes to our attention through no fault of our own. An officemate might send you the link, or will be viewing it (and laughing like a loon) when you pass by. The point is that sometimes distractions are shown to us by other people, and though it is not their intention to make your productivity drop, it ends up doing so. That's why you will need to stay on track and avert your eyes. When you're done with work, then you can amuse yourself to no end, right?

57 Don't download and install with abandon.

Practice Internet safety to avoid infection. It's all too easy to abuse the Internet provided by your office. Downloading programs and the like, you're basically getting them for free. Matters of piracy aside, downloading and installing programs downloaded from less-than-reputable sites can introduce viral infections to your terminal. The effects range from unnoticeable to rapid decline in performance and breakdown. If you use a computer when working and it breaks down, you lose precious time to the required repairs, and worse, you get busted for downloading and installing things that are not contributive to your work.

58 Don't stream videos or download using the company bandwidth.

If you work in a corporate environment that does not apply bandwidth limitations per terminal, then you shouldn't stream videos or download material from the Web. Aside from being construable as improper use of company resources, you risk slowing the network down for everyone because of the bandwidth you are consuming.

59 Don't visit websites other than reference and work-related websites.

Banning any and all unauthorized websites is difficult in practice for companies, so they would rather apply policies by informing the employees. If you're one such employee, you should follow those policies and not visit unauthorized websites. Leave your online shopping, sports news, or titillating images for when you are at home. Additionally, you should know that some companies monitor the websites you visit via the network nodes, so erasing your browser history usually isn't of much help. Being caught simply visiting the wrong website can get you fired from your job.

60 Don't socialize during work.

One of the biggest distractions during work is socializing with coworkers. While there is nothing inherently wrong with this, remember that your main focus should be your job. Any talks with people in the office should be restricted to work-related topics – not the latest office gossip. Remember that it does not take a lot to ruin your momentum. If you really want to catch up with your coworkers, do so in your own time. There is always the time after work and the weekend to fulfill all your social needs.

61 Don't meet someone out of the blue.

You may not realize it but having a sudden meeting with someone can ruin your productivity and waste your time. Such meetings are only good for interrupting your train of thought and disturbing your concentration. Next time a coworker drops by at your desk and starts some chit-chat, politely suggest meeting him or her at a time that is convenient to both of you. You would be surprised to find out how much time you waste in these idle and unimportant chats.

Things To Do After Work

Your work does not really end after you finish it. As paradoxical as that statement is, there is truth in it. There are things that you can do after completing tasks to improve productivity. Yes, you may be tired already, but try to do these as much as possible, okay?

62 Put away your tools and equipment.

You might be using them again as soon as you start the next day, but that is no excuse for leaving them lying about. Putting away your tools and equipment does not just keep them organized, it also makes the work area safer, and in the case of common resources, makes it easy for others to find and use them. Also, if someone has sticky fingers, putting away your tools can secure them so you don't lose productivity by trying to search for something which is no longer there.

63 Shut down your computer.

Some people simply put their computers into sleep mode or let them run overnight with the monitor turned off. Unless you are running some resource-heavy task that requires all night, you should shut down your computer. Putting a computer into sleep or hibernate mode does not allow it to flush its memory completely, which means that you don't get off to a fresh start when you turn it on the next day. A full shutdown means that you can start off from the best possible state because your computer was able to clean itself with the shutdown.

64 If you need to leave your computer running, turn off the monitor and use an automatic shutdown application.

Sometimes we can't wait for our computers to complete certain tasks, which is why we sometimes need to leave them running after hours. If you want to do so, make sure you turn off the monitor and set an automatic shutdown. Give your shutdown a little leeway in case the task takes a little longer than expected.

65 Tidy up your workspace.

When you're done for the day, make sure to tidy up your workspace. Place papers in folders or envelopes. Pick up bits of trash and throw them into the waste bin. Wash your coffee mug. Do what you can to improve the cleanliness and orderliness of your area so you can come in the next day to a neat and conducive workplace.

66 Lock up.

Lock up what you can if it is under your jurisdiction to do so (i.e. you have the keys). Whether it is your desk drawers, a document safe, windows, or doors, you should make sure that they are locked as you leave the workplace. Security is essential to productivity, as it ensures that you won't be set back by losses in supplies, equipment, end-products, or vital documents.

67 Review your work at the end of the day.

More specifically, take time to analyze how you did things afterwards. Maybe there is a more efficient way of finishing your report that you have yet to stumble upon. You will never know if there is a better way of doing things unless you start looking for one. If there happens to be one, throw out your old habit and adapt a better strategy. Do not be afraid to try new things especially if it might bring better results or optimize your work process. You will only thank yourself later.

68 Pat yourself on the back.

There are times when all you need is some good old encouragement. When you do well enough, your boss or supervisor is bound to take notice and compliment you for a job well done. Who says you cannot do this for yourself? At the end of a grueling day, why not pat yourself on the back and congratulate yourself for finishing everything? This kind of self-encouragement is great for your self-confidence as well as your overall well-being. End your day the same way you started it – in a good mood.

Things To Do In General

This section covers the tips that don't quite fall into any of the above categories, but are nonetheless useful in helping you achieve a higher level of productivity.

69 Find a way to unwind after work.

Everyone needs to have an outlet, preferably something constructive. Stress from our jobs makes live in general more difficult, and our jobs more dislikable. This stress builds up unless there is some way to release it. A good hobby can relieve the stress, making it easier to stick with the job. It lowers those "I hate my job" feelings, enabling you to perform your tasks more efficiently. If your hobby produces some form of product, whether physical or digital, you could also sell it for incidental income.

70 Put some good music on.

Music calms the wildest beast and the same goes true with a disorganized mind. Science has already proven the calming effects of certain kinds of music. When the opportunity allows for such, pop some earphones on and listen to good music for a change. It is certainly a welcome change and break from the usual office conversations and staccato humming of the office fax machine. Good music is great for clearing your head and helping you concentrate more. Just make sure that you are not disturbing the person next to you. He or she may not like your preference of music after all.

71 Get out of bed before the rest of the world.

Setting your alarm clock at least an hour earlier then everyone else's is great for getting you to work early in the morning. Apart from keeping you from showing up late, it allows for some time alone in the office. No phone calls, no one dropping by at your desk and other such things. In other words, you have the office to yourself with virtually no distractions. Quite obviously, this boosts productivity by allowing you to concentrate on the task at hand.

72 Do not drink your stress away.

Lots of people seek relief from stress by drinking, often to excess. While the infrequent drink with friends is fine and a glass of wine with dinner is nice, drinking to get rid of problems causes more problems in itself. Alcohol is not the solution to your work stress, or any stress for that matter. Drinking is at its best when done as a social activity with discipline and moderation, at least in terms of amount consumed.

73 Perform regular maintenance on all tools and equipment.

Whether you work with socket wrenches or on a computer terminal, you should perform regular maintenance. Oil hinges. Dust air inlets and outlets. Wipe down surfaces. Run a defragmenter. Perform full system scans. Create restore points. Check for leaks. Walk around and check if everything's safe and secure. Whatever it is that you do for a living there is something you can do to maintain good working conditions.

74 Find out if anything's expired.

This one applies mostly to those who work in food-related or pharmaceutical jobs. Lots of consumables have expiration dates, and if you don't go through your inventory regularly, you risk leaving expired items on the shelf for buyers to pick out and buy. This can lead to a lot of problems, so it is best to check regularly for expired items and to remove them from the shelves or avoid using them.

75 Check for discrepancies in inventory.

A regular inventory audit can reveal discrepancies in inventory and reported sales volumes. This can lead to investigations into pilferage, shoplifting, or simply bad accounting. Whatever the result may be, there is always something you can do to make it better.

76 Mix in with the right crowd.

The sad truth is that not everyone works productively. Some just lounge off and get by with the bare minimum. To really help boost your productivity, surround yourself with like-minded people who are really into what they are doing. If you can, work with people who have the same work habits and styles as you do. Laid back people are better off working with the same happy-go-lucky crowd. If you are someone who would rather be serious, find someone else who shares this ideal. This helps sync up your work habits and produces a harmonious relationship with your coworkers.

77 Perform financial audits.

Aside from possibly discovering embezzlement and pilferages, performing regular financial audits enables you to better understand your business's performance. Productivity is also about making the most of what you have, and you can't make the most of what you have if some of it goes missing.

78 Find time to exercise.

Regular exercise not only keeps your body fir but your mind sharp as well. You already spend eight hours of your life sitting on a chair on the weekdays. Break this routine on the weekends and start getting up more. No need to build your body here. Just spend one to hours a day at the gym to get your heart pumping and your blood flowing. Exercising on the weekend also helps break the monotony of work and helps get rid of the Monday blues when it is time to work again.

79 Get some well-deserved R & R.

There is a reason why they say "work hard, play harder." After a rough week at the office, it is best to pat yourself on the back with some good old rest and recreation. Find time to do something you want like watching the football game or firing up the barbecue. Anything that helps clear your mind for the week ahead is a great thing to do. The main point here is to relax and free yourself from stress and you are going to need it. So put your feet up and unwind until it is time for work again.

80 Get enough sleep.

Staying up all night then going to work the next day is never a good idea. A lack of sleep will most surely decrease your attention span and your ability to concentrate. Of course this is bad news for productivity. So instead of being up all night, do not go past your bed time. It is a bit juvenile but it does help in bringing your brain to work mode the following day. This way, you are not a slave to the coffee machine anymore. Keep your mind fresh and up to the task and you will soon have better output.

81 Make yourself comfortable.

It is no secret that comfort brings the mind to a better state where concentration is at its finest. You simply cannot expect someone to come up with a breakthrough in uncomfortable situations. So get an ergonomic chair, wear a sweater vest to keep yourself warm or turn up the air conditioning. Anything that can be done to make you feel comfortable while working should be done without delay. It is for the best after all.

82 Stay "electronic."

If you are a highly mobile worker who spends as much time working in the plane, you are much better off keeping electronic copies of all the files you need. The last thing you need is to shuffle through scores of papers while on a trip. Keeping soft copies of your paperwork also reduces the weight you have to bring along. If you must take down notes for a meeting, keep a small notebook handy. Otherwise, everything should be saved in a flash thumb drive. This may need some getting used to during the first few trips but it is well worth the adjustment you have to go through.

Things That Home-Based Workers Can Do

Modern advances in technology have created a new breed of employee – the home-based worker. As the name suggests, they work from the comforts of their own home more often than not as freelancers. New they may be but they also face a few challenges of their own – some unique, others all too familiar. This section is dedicated to tips on how to improve productivity at home offices.

83 Establish a routine.

More often than not, the main problem of working from home is procrastination. There are simply too many distractions lying about. Since you do not have a work schedule, you will have to come up with one yourself. Only by implementing a work schedule can you lessen procrastination and thus improve productivity from home. When the time for work comes, the brain can quickly shift into gear and you will feel more inclined to work. Do this everyday and you have yourself a classic work routine where everything that needs to be done is done as second nature.

84 Find out when you are most ready for work.

Home-based workers are not necessarily working in 9 to 5 shifts. There is no need to stick to this time frame either. Some choose to work in the morning while others wait until nightfall. The important thing to consider here is when you feel like working. It is one important advantage that working from home has. Use this to your own advantage by setting up your work schedule to coincide with the time frame you are most likely at your most productive. Just make sure that it is a fixed time frame you will stick to everyday.

85 Plan ahead of work.

Home-based workers often get different workloads throughout the work week. This makes it a bit more difficult to plan the day ahead. Nevertheless, it is best to work based on a schedule even a tentative one. This way, you have an idea on how to go about the day and lets you accomplish what needs to done right off the bat. This makes procrastination and confusion less likely. It also serves as your plan of action which you can always consult whenever you seem to be lost and in need of guidance.

86 Itemize your workload.

Reading off the work for the day is often daunting and makes you want to not work at all. When this happens, you can always turn to an age-old solution – the to-do list. Having a to-do list lets you organize your work load and checking items off as you go is also encouraging. Online tools that can help you create such a list do exist. Still, you have the option of coming up with one from the ground up. To-do lists have been proven effective at clearing your head and preparing it for work so do not underestimate its power. It may as well be the answer you are looking for.

87 Tell friends and family that you are on work mode.

Working from home is a relatively new phenomenon that some people still fail to grasp. As such, some friends and family tend to downplay the seriousness of your work. "You are not even in an office" as they often quip. Unfortunately, this does not distractions from friends and family which is bad when you are trying to catch up on a deadline. When this happens, it is best to make them aware that you are working and cannot afford to be distracted. Explain to them that you are not free just because you are at home.

88 Focus but not on social networking sites.

In home offices where internet access is virtually unrestricted, distraction from such sites as Facebook and Twitter is all too common. When not needed, it is best to disconnect from your router or broadband connection. Creative tasks such as designing and writing will benefit greatly from this. You will be amazed at how much time you can recover when you start focusing on the work at hand. Once you are done, you will have all the time you want to start chatting and browsing the internet once again. For now, you have to focus.

89 Track your progress.

With no boss around, it is up to you to check on your own progress. Check the actual work you have done against the current time. Did you take longer or faster than you expected? This should give you a good idea if you are being productive or not. You can track your progress manually or with help from software called RescueTime. This is an online time-tracking software which tells its user how he or she spends his or her time on the computer. It really helps time your tasks so consider it as an investment for increased productivity and better output.

90 Set-up a home office or a separate space for work.

Working out of your bedroom or in front of the TV is no good especially if you want to be productive. As such, you want to devote a separate space for work to make a distinction between work and play. As much as possible, find a quiet space in your home where there will not be so much distraction. Get all the hardware you need and put it in one convenient place for quick and easy access. Having a home office is best but any spot where you can work quietly is good enough.

91 Outsource some of the work.

Business owners who find it difficult to fit everything needed into an already hectic schedule. Most business people make the mistake of thinking they can do something themselves to cut costs. On the other hand, the time wasted is really not worth it. With this in mind, you are better off hiring a messenger, virtual assistant, bookkeeper and others to do the job for you. Automate as much of your process as possible so you do not have to worry much. This frees up your mind from mundane tasks so you can have more brilliant ideas.

92 Buddy up and check on each other.

Some people just do not have enough self-discipline to keep them working. If you are like that, you are better off getting a work buddy to check on you from time to time. Ideally, this should be someone who tracks your progress and gives suggestions on how to improve your productivity. Collaborate with a friend online and help each other out. Essentially, you are asking him or her to act like your boss. As much as possible, ask help from someone who works from home as well.

93 Invest in sound and reliable technology.

Working from home means less in-person meetings for you. Still, the importance of such meetings is present. As such, most of your work is conducted over the phone and/or online. Investing in the best technology money can buy is a good idea then. Some printers can now double as a photocopy and even a fax machine so do look into those. It may cost more but it will give off better benefits in the long run. Simple services such as voice mail and call waiting are a huge help as well.

94 Modern conveniences are your best friends.

In relation to the previous tip, the home-based worker also needs to be aware of modern technologies that can make life easier. A smartphone is ideal for entrepreneurs on the go where you can check your email and make and receive phone calls anytime, anywhere. The latest high-performance laptops have enough computing power for applications needed by graphic designers. A fast broadband connection lets you finish your tasks quickly and without delay. Consider what you need to get the job done and invest your money accordingly. Your clients will only thank you with their continued patronage.

95 Take frequent and short breaks.

Just like working in the office, working at home also requires short breaks in between. Be sure to at least close your eyes for at least five minutes every hour. This reduces the strain caused by staring at the computer all day. You can also try walking around to stretch your legs a bit. Grab a quick snack to help replenish your energy and keep your mind sharp and active. You can even lie down for a while to get your bearing straight. Just be careful not to doze off completely!

96 Dress for the occasion.

Just because you are working at home does not mean you get to wear your pajamas to work. Well you can but that is not a good idea. Working in your pajamas just encourages you to slack off and doze off. Continue your routine as you would when you were still going to the office. Wake up, shower, brush your teeth, get dressed and eat breakfast as you normally would. You do not have to change in that respect in the first place. In other words, continue behaving like the model employee that you are.

97 If you are not up to it, STOP.

This may seem counter-productive but consider this: you have been staring at a blinking cursor for hours but no words seem to come to mind. Take this as a sign that you are not ready to work yet. When this happens, find something else to do until you feel like working again. Just do not over indulge yourself. The point here is to refresh your mind in an effort to jumpstart it to work mode. Be sure that you are still meeting the deadlines you have set though.

98 Quantity or quality?

Another thing that home-based workers should be mindful of is the quality of their work. With no one else to check and proofread, it is easy for quality to get left behind the dust. Combine this with procrastination and cramming and you have a recipe for disaster. While you are working, it is best to check for the quality of your article, design or whatever it is you are working on. At the end of the day ask yourself one important question, "Is this the kind of work I want my clients to think I am capable of?"

99 Do not burn yourself out.

At the extreme end of procrastination is working your self too hard. Just because you can work 12 to 14 hours in a day does not mean you should. It may be tempting to "do tomorrow's work today for a free day after" but it must be avoided. Over time, the quality of your work begins to deteriorate resulting in poor results. Working long hours is only bad for productivity. So do yourself a favor and take a break every now and then. Work within your capabilities and avoid overstretching yourself.

100 Get a change of scenery.

Working and living in the same location can drive someone mad. This is the most common problem that home-based workers face on a daily basis which is often bad for productivity. The best way to address this problem is to get out of the house and find a nice place to work in. Coffee shops are your best bet but libraries might be better because of the environment. Alternatively, you can try relaxing on the beach while you work. Nothing beats the warm ocean breeze and fresh air as you write your article or come up with a new design.

101 Suit yourself.

The beauty of working at home is that you can adapt your environment as you see fit. Want music? Turn on the radio or your iPod. Want to be more comfortable? Sit on the couch and type away with your laptop on hand. Want to eat while working? Head on to the kitchen and make yourself a sandwich. It is so easy to work according to your own wishes when you work at home. Use this to your advantage and set-up an environment that encourages you to work harder and produce better results.

Conclusion

As you can see from all the tips given here, being more productivity at work does not always mean making drastic changes. Everything you learned here requires small changes on your part. These are things you can certainly do.

Different these tips may be, all of them have one thing in common. These tips will only work as long as you act on them. That is, if you start including these in your work habit, you are bound to see the results you are looking for. Reading and learning about it is just one part of the equation.

With this in mind, you want to start improving your productivity and boosting your performance as soon as possible. Keep in mind that it is up to you to make the difference. So what are you waiting for? Work better and start to impress your boss, client or coworkers. You will never know when you are next in line for a promotion.

www.ingramcontent.com/pod-product-compliance
Lightning Source LLC
LaVergne TN
LVHW020455080526
838202LV00057B/5969